TREE OF HEAVEN

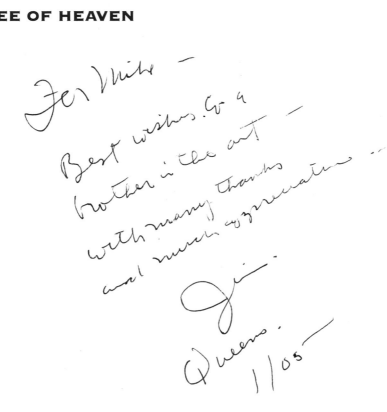

For Mike —

Best wishes to a
brother in the art —
with many thanks
and much appreciation —

Jim.

Queens.
1/05

Winner of the Iowa Poetry Prize

TREE OF HEAVEN

Poems by James McKean

University of Iowa Press Ψ Iowa City

University of Iowa Press,

Iowa City 52242

Copyright © 1995 by James McKean

Printed in the United States

of America

Printed on acid-free paper

Library of Congress

Cataloging-in-Publication Data

McKean, James, 1946–

    Tree of heaven: poems / by James

    McKean.

       p.   cm. – (Iowa poetry prize)

  ISBN 0-87745-505-8

  I. Title. II. Series.

  PS3563.C3737T7   1995

  811′.54 – dc20   94-49018

                             CIP

01 00 99 98 97 96   P 5 4 3 2

FOR MY FATHER

CONTENTS

ACKNOWLEDGMENTS

Grateful acknowledgment is made to the editors of the following magazines in which these poems first appeared.

Antioch Review: "Les Grues"

Cincinnati Poetry Review: "The Try-Your-Strength Machine at the Tivoli Gardens" and "Splitting Wood"

Gettysburg Review: "Rider" and "Your Leaving"

High Plains Literary Review: "Whale Rock"

The Journal: "Rowboat" and "This Way, Please"

Kenyon Review: "House Wrens"

Nimrod: "Concert," "Quarry," and "Snow Angel"

Plum Review: "Fireflies" and "First Snow"

Poetry Northwest: "Breakneck," "Dead Reckoning," and "Reunion, Cannon Beach"

Prairie Schooner: "A Story after Dinner," "Silver Thaw," and "Two Magpies"

Seneca Review: "A Hawk in the Yard," "The Ride Back," and "Whispering in Leo Kauf's Ear"

Special thanks to James McCorkle and Jan Weissmiller.

FIREFLIES

Too slow means a fast end,
a heavy hand, a jar
with holes punched in the lid,
a gathering of children
around the lights,
a milling of Chinese lanterns.
Cupped in my hand
one light fills my eye perfectly.
All evening I sit
on the porch swing and watch
not knowing where
the next will turn up – heat
lightning too far away
to hear. Across the street in a window
upstairs a light leads
children to bed. How
like us to work for one encounter
or nothing and wander
our whole lives, dragging a lamp
that gives us away.

PART ONE

SOW BEAR

We are thankful
for our side of the river
and the blue-green cold and the stones
ice-dropped where we stand
and watch the sow bear
in her midsummer fat, rummage
for roots or sockeye,
her great brown haunches toward us.
When she looks back,
we are thankful once more
that the river sweeps away the meaning
for "rival." We are nothing –
not food nor fear nor stink
of much interest and
it's her choice, thank you, how
little to make of us,
numb-footed and crazy
from too much light these long days.
Oh, blessèd indifference!
Behind a stump, a bough of spruce,
we're once-overed and dis-
missed, not worth a woof or a charge
for which we are thankful again, empty-handed,
and lousy, we admit,
at planning for winter, dreamers
on two feet forever,
who see a bear even after she's gone
and the wind follows her
flower by flower through the white
cow parsley.

TEACHING CANARIES HOW TO SING

We're too far north,
and the afternoon outside my window sets
too soon for wild canaries,
singer of harsh songs
my grandmother would have said.
I remember my uncle told me one day,
don't let on she's dying,
but the moment I saw the light behind her
I knew she knew and wouldn't
speak of it, would rather gab with me
in bad Spanish, a new tense
she'd invent for tomorrow:
I will go to Guadalajara
by Greyhound and sit in the square
of roses in the sun and read
beneath a large hat a story of beautiful cages.

Afraid, I spoke of cuttlebone,
the open-mouth Victrola she wound
until the perfect canary sang
and all her birds listened to a song
they already knew. She said no,
to speak of my future,
a trip now like this one south
on a train slow up the grade of anonymous
backlit mountains where a child
she never knew sleeps, a woman reads,
my own face looks back,
as if this reflection in the window

were a cage to sing from:
I will go to Guadalajara.
I will sit in the square of roses in the sun
and read beneath a large hat
a story of beautiful cages,
of canaries that sing for all
they cannot have.

TELL ME,

what does *esperanza* mean and why
do so many unmarried daughters
live here by that name?
To the north a whistle in the black
night moonless beyond
the stone walls of the house
in Guadalajara I try to sleep in.
Under the roof of this retired
railroad engineer, his Avon
door-to-door saleswoman wife
wants me to stay forever, I can tell –
to the south another whistle
in answer – how? The food, the long
line of relatives, my own room,
a luxury. She said, sleep,
sleep, but I have too much to rid
myself of. Words for one,
words I wasn't born with but learned
before I knew I'd learned them,
cockroaches for another, the fear
I mean, and my imagining
a murder next door just this morning –
another whistle close by
then one far away. Why all these
revolvers and red lights,
this sobbing I can't get out of my ears?
I can't sleep. The bed's too
short, the hot water's off one minute
after prayers. Tell me,

what does *esperanza* mean?
Tell me, who claims the dark all night
with rickety bikes and new
shiny whistles?

THIS WAY, PLEASE

Restaurante El Coral

Don't feed the dogs.
Sit and eat. That's better. Sorry.
Our sign points
wrong, an old nail's
fault. There is nothing
the way you came but
thin soil and bridges built
in the mind of someone
who lives in the city. We see
your shirt bleeds, your new
leather shoes wet
from blisters. Don't worry.
The tide returns
at ten. Sit here.
Never mind the pig
tiptoeing over her teats.
She suspects you foul
the air and worries
about her children. Her tattoo
means "tomorrow." Never mind
old men who stuff
their pockets full
of sparrows. Children
who swim through the air.
Your fish is boned.
The beer is warm
but still Carta Blanca.

Another? Soon. Please,
feed only yourself.
The lame mustard-colored dog
you pity with scraps
cannot stand up
to being murdered.
It must eat in secret.
Here's the wolf now,
a good dog for killing the lame.
Patience. His work
takes only a minute, only a life.
There are many dogs
and so few tourists.
You have come a long way
to tolerate the wind
at your table. You must
eat before you pay
and drink, yes, drink
before you walk the short way back
where every shell you find
not crushed by waves
is yours to keep.

THE PLACE OF MOSQUITOES

Punta Mita

We cannot stay here,
Martinez says, cutting the engine to coast.
Deaf, we might never leave,
stumbling knee-deep,
bled dry by the dark prayer
of appetite. Where are we,
hypnotized by humid air
as cool and thick as fog?
We see ourselves in water
silver beneath the anaqua trees,
their leaves folding up light
so only shadow falls,
so air-breathing orchids bloom
only if the light
we bring stirs them. Here,
white petals – a rose-spotted pendulous lip
like a mouth cradling
its delicate fangs. Yes. Please.
I want to stop and kneel.
I want to lie down in mud
and sleep the succulent sleep
of leaves until my eyes
unfold, until I slip into wings,
a white silk moth lifting
in a shower of dust
and light and choirs singing.
Do you hear it? Something from long ago

I will never find –
a voice so faint and calling now
I find myself, when the engine starts,
slapping at my ears.

WHISPERING IN LEO KAUF'S EAR

A statue of Leo Kauf, noted industrialist, sits in a town square,
and each morning people wait in line to whisper in his ear.

Daylight winds through the Plaza Dos Almas
where children don't believe in turns but get one
anyway, breaking the tail of some lame dog – oh, such sins,
such peccadillos. Remember? Our thoughtlessness,
our strangling another living thing? And for what?
I thought so. If only we could talk things away,
we'd haul our dead upright to wait patient in the sun,
smelling the oil of breakfast, the flurry
of pigeons at their crumbs. But now as if put off
by the lame, the dour pigeon-toed young woman,
the old man's north-of-the-border suit and stingy coin
he lays in the bronze hand that never moves,
we fidget. In line again. Come to take ourselves back
if someone would listen. Listen. Each word
repairs the ear. He knows our story, waits all day
for its predictably sad and open-ended ending,
and expects nothing. So, what are we to say to an emptiness
where all talk is small and echoes?
What are we to say to sympathy that shines
for so many confessions distilled to whispers and poured
into a sober ear? Come now. What will we say
when nothing is worse for its saying, the line behind us now
as we bend to this lustered ear,
our notes whistling through his hollow skull.

THE RIDE BACK

After a line by Rilke

Before me there is no sleep
as deep as the first color of evening,
no bath like the red light
leaching the trees to flat nothing.
One day we gave our spare to a stranger
who paid us in opium, what he had,
and the black tar bubbled all the way
our car drove us somehow home.
We saw instant nostalgia – a sweet inhalation
of memory before the squint-eyed
traffic, before the white concrete abrasion,
before the sun that set later
and later. And now dropping back
into a solution of memory and dreams –
the car once more even and habitual,
the way home the same way home, four walls
standing still as I knew them,
the door opening, the walk's wet stones,
the trees grown away from me,
gritty and tight-fisted all winter,
about to let go their buds – are words.
There will be no more opium tar, tin foil, smoking
ourselves into the colors of dawn.

ROWBOAT

Afloat, oars up
in summer, in eddies beside fallen trees
and limestone laid down in dust,
we drift ten feet offshore.
Water gives way. We do
nothing but displace our weight
and leave the shore behind,
nothing but lift hands before our eyes
and drop them before the fox,
an accident of silence
and drifting, his color gotten from
another season's leaves.
Such black eyes lying out of reach.
He gives nothing back
but ourselves suspended, nothing but nerves
unmoved as if at last
we belong to a moment held
by water and air, as if
he is true sleep and we awake
floating in the light
of afternoon until words rise up,
nothing more than "look" and "over there,"
as if pointing might pin
the moment to our sleeve,
as if to say "here," that little wake of air
rolling onto shore.

WORRY DOLLS

They are what we turn to
when we turn away,
when we speak of nothing
to no one one humid
evening gone stubborn
with sorrow. How wide-eyed
is their wonder,
how ageless their grins.
And when we doubt the good
of speaking our most
desperate thoughts,
or whether anyone
ever hears our language
of grief, thin
at the sleeve, the cloak
of a mother's voice
outgrown and faded,
they listen. That's it.
What more is this
but a moment's bow
to what we don't know
beyond the little we do?
What more but a few words
to fit us, to dress
what we fear might be
nothing, nothing at all?

HERON

A blue heron fell
out of its wings, folded
them and stands still this morning
on reverse knees, neck
extended, saber beak point
to point with the water's own replica
of heron. I can't wait.
The sky whitens.
I remember evening,
my lying against the gunwale of a skiff,
drifting toward an island's
chatter of birds. I would have stayed
forever in the sun-falling
and held the hand that reached up
toward mine and drifted
but for whispering in the air, eyes
turned down toward me
before wings and yellow legs trailing. It was time.
In long strokes I rowed
toward a fire onshore, smoke drifting
over water, over me – and oh,
the heron strikes
and raises something up this morning
that shines.

THE NIGHT BEFORE A MORNING'S FISHING

I should sleep or find
something to say
to the blank-faced sea.
Spoons and spinners
and Eagleclaws –
I say these names as
if my voice might
cast the lie that salmon
need to strike and
run themselves to exhaustion.
I tie up hooks – five
turns, the line back
through, cinched on the eye –
and kiss the knot
for luck's sake, for my
father once more
up the night before
his morning's fishing,
windows dark, the tide
book open, hooks
whetted until they score
the moon rising
in his nail like
candlefish boiling up,
a King not far
below, called by his
"Fish, fish, fish,"
the closest I ever heard him
come to singing
before another day began.

YOUR LEAVING

Was that a door
set into its jamb, the latch bolt
falling the moment we chose to worry
a button loose or turn
at a sound outside across the road,
a dog barking at someone
leaning down through a fence and stepping
into a field? It isn't you
no matter what we wish and the field
lies fallow and unnamed.
From small towns we came to sit beside you
and straighten your bed
and argue ten ways to say a simple thing.
We rubbed your cold feet
and counted the places we had never been
and would never go because
we were afraid to name the next choice
in our lives. But you waited
and when we woke early from fitful sleep,
our places lost in books open
for the vigil we could not keep, you gathered
your things in the morning dark
and giving the matter
no more thought as if you had heard us say
OK and we'll be fine,
you left and there was a pressure in our ears
as if a door had closed,
and we stood on our feet and held each other
and turned the lamp down
to gather the light around us.

LAVA FLOW, WAHAULA

For Penny

That the red moment we come to
in steam before the sea
exploding and black sand
raining down upon the new shore – simple
and bare – is not ours.
Some long wearing away later
in a slower burning
we might rename the bed we lie on,
the warmth between us and
having spoken, rise and walk back
through too many steps to count,
the wind in our faces.
But today, hands in our pockets,
we must touch nothing
to keep our luck. To be touched
and glad to find our own way
back into the cold.

ICE

Ice stops the river beneath
the wind's deflection of light,
too thin where I cross

only in thinking. See breath made clear,
a lung-full of air ladled
into the night. See words backlit

by the moon, broken. Listen,
it is foolish to try and read
the current's hand.

What's acceptable?
An inch? A foot? We cross
in the dark under a moon frozen,

the willow before us all white lace as if
breath had hung the branches in vows.
Ice speaks only to itself,

all unrest, unheld, a thought sketched
freehand. Far off, buildings
steam, the night settled on enterprise

and wash rags laid on the foreheads
of children, frost edging
its way across locked windows: a crystal

stammer. Lamps on a steel
bridge above us flutter in wind drifts. Below,
the moon goes to pieces and suffers

the loss of water. Silence.
Easy our walking between sky and water
here on the stopped river

that drives us on, clamping
and tired. And then the bridge
we return over rings

brittle with sand
and spot welding. The willow
we leave behind trails

branches like damage.
On this ridiculous night, on a bridge
we cross halfway to stare

at water caught
in midsentence, bullied by the cold,
I close my eyes on

another reasonable excuse.
And when I wake, hunched into my shoulders,
I see in a far building

a man and woman talk,
and when she turns to her hands, frowning,
and then outside, as if

her reflection looks back
stunned from the other side of glass,
I know she decides

on an old future.
No, I say to no one near.
Reach down through a hole cut in ice, yes, there,

and trail a hand, the warmth beneath
hidden before another thaw,
sheets stacked beside concrete pillars

this bridge rides on. Here,
beside the traffic you wish for steaming its way home,
here something must move in hazy sound.

PART TWO

SKIN TEST

It comes back:
my mother's incessant washing,
the backyard line set in flapping sheets,
her disposition scrubbed clean
of patience as she rose from stooping
to find my day's discovery tracked across her
brilliant floor. No words

stood up to the switching, her finger
shaken beneath my nose that late summer
I remember full of evening
sun and voices heard through my room's tattered
yellow shade. "Come out,
wherever you are."

I could go back
no longer skinny. I could rest
as I was told. I could speak of the forbidden,
the money in her hands
as she paid my best friend to rake her leaves.
How I wrestled him to tears and deadlock,
shamed by what

she hadn't allowed.
How I stole coins from her, wrong
about what was fair, wrong about her anger
as she scrubbed my back
each evening to wash the TB swelling away.
I could go back, a peddler
of better soap, a witness to the possibility

of a future, confessing
what I couldn't then – how I waited, against her orders,
outside Hamlin Park Sanatorium,
my best friend's mother
pale behind her window and Kleenex,
mumbling words

I couldn't hear.
I could let it go. The spot on my back
has healed though "Sorry" still flutters down
like indecipherable leaves
gathered and dry, a gift I bring each year, shoes
in hand for my mother's
clean, clean floor.

WHALE ROCK

Where is our consolation? – Robinson Jeffers
Big Sur

The road no-shouldered,
I worried around each
hairpin, sure I was that rich
and vulgar civilization,
dying at the core, bewildered,
eager to witness something larger,
more peaceful than myself.
And when the hitchhiker pointed,
I held my breath. I saw the dark
flukes, the jaw barnacled,
and one eye cleansing my own.
But when the woman who sold me gas
said this whale never moves,
I saw how illusions
are given to the eager.
From the gorge-cut hills, from the waves
I held until they broke too far down
even to hear, I saved words
for the road back out,
the gray rolling in.

LES GRUES

Today it's face to face,
not my eyes-straight-ahead walk,
Pigalle metro stop as fast as I can past
the half-open Dutch door
two buildings up from the safe, green
garden of Hotel Navarone.

For five days I've suffered hoots
and black stockings. I blamed
my hat, my solidly critical chin,
indignity rising in my cheeks
like cheap *vin rosé*. Calm, calm,
I kept saying, these gibes

shall pass like smoke out the half-door,
guffaws as cobbled as the street
I hurried up on, the daily
stuck under my arm, ridicule the price
I paid for predictable habits,
for walking this street and not living

here – such lessons
in how to stand out in a crowd.
But today they're proud, all
congratulations. I copy a master,
the great knight errant
bowing page after page humbly

before his *altas damas*.
Today I sport a new suit and raise

my hands, hat falling off
the moment I lean too far over the half-door:
cigarettes drop from open mouths,
then cheers then whistles

then applause, of course, as I gargle
in bad French, *Vive les grues* –
boas rustling in blue light
as I praise their brilliant feathers,
their stately walk, oh,
how fine they look in flight.

THE TRY-YOUR-STRENGTH MACHINE
AT THE TIVOLI GARDENS

So here I am, surprised
how little my decision weighs,
how heavy the wooden-headed hammer
seems. Three swings at one
kroner each and with each
swing another show-off
shown up, all grunt and good
intentions falling far – in
embarrassed silence – short. So what
if my first swing is nothing
but gravity, a slip,
a poke and a hanging on,
and so what if my second, full-
fledged honest effort seems
only so-so, a humph's
worth maybe or at worst a giggle's.
Take this: a lung-
blistered, gill and reptilian
three-quarter circle swing and crush,
dust pummeled in a near
miss of foot and leg
but a direct hit on the stone
and brick setup and support
where iron frameworks
not meant for drop-forging lie
bent by the now split wooden-headed,
handle-cracked mallet.
So there's no bell. No Kewpie doll.

The crowd's disgusted
but my girl's pleased and the carny's
so tickled he finds a new mallet
so I might have one more
on-the-house and dangerous prize-
winning swing.

HOUSE WRENS

Troglodytes aedon

The day the wrens moved in
I found myself master
of nothing. All the plans
I'd laid – mitered
corners, pitched roof, the door
hole small enough to keep out
rotund sparrows –
why, all my painstaking ladder-
climbing, sun-plotted placement
for shade and shelter
ten feet up the south side
of my barn
               went to ingrates.
I know what I expected.
I know what I got:
suspicion, scolds, pinwheeling
flybys and songs that meant "back off,"
as if I were some squat-
minded starling.
             Suffer
the little children it says
and I did. Grudged
nuisance status in the greening
spring, binoculared,
I wished to help in their nesting,
sold on that simple model
for a life – food, offspring, someplace

out of the rain.
                   When they
left for good, I cleaned the twigs out
until the wren house lay
vacant above me, their keeper,
who makes way for what the seasons
bring – birds with comic
names too big to fly away with,
those exquisite wrens, those egg-breakers
from the beginning.

BREAKNECK

In your case a fracture
of the third cervical vertebra,
but for me, the cousin
who never kept up,
it was fear squeezing
my eyes shut as we freewheeled
two on your bike down
the steepest hill in Lynnwood,
your mother's words
"You'll break your necks,"
dying in the wind
behind us. What comes
to mind are casts and splints
and ragged Ace bandages
unwinding from the normal
contusions we both suffered,
but you more somehow,
summer after spring after winter
after fall as if danger
was the full measure
of air your lungs needed,
as if only something
broken or bruised or scraped
convinced you, yes,
here is the line, the limit,
the point of no return
you returned to time and again
either swinging on frayed
ropes or jumping house

to tree to ground or leaping,
eyes straight ahead,
fifty feet into water so shallow
your feet itched for weeks
before you broke the casts
off with a hammer.
And finally, your sledding down
Mt. Rainier, headfirst, that
late-night call and the next day
my father holding me up
to watch you lie absolutely
still, sand bags at the end of a rope
pulling your head straight.
How did your mother know?
It's a wonder we grew up,
but we did — I falling
for the prophecy of words
like *breakneck* and *bad luck*,
and you out of your steel halo
and into the Marines,
your neck fused into permanent
attention so even if
you wanted to, you told them,
you'd never look down.

FAKE ID

Once I was the biggest
and elected to wear the watch cap and pea coat
and carry the rare birth certificate and
discharge papers – "Chuck Luna,"
I read and folded them into my pocket and stood
by the Dumpster behind Frank and Mike's Tavern, sweating
on a slow Thursday afternoon.
Rumors led us here, sixteen-year-olds,
to buy beer, to eat boiled eggs, to shoot pool behind the big window
we'd only looked through
sidelong from the sidewalk, walking past, figuring.
Not breathing through the galvanized
back door I tipped, no, sauntered past the sour
men's room, the rack of bent cues,
ashtrays full on the empty
chairs beside the felt-ripped pool table
and searched the haze
for one vacant red-vinyl, duct-taped bar stool
to climb like a witness, weary
and sullen after my newly invented two years
at sea, breaking ice in Barrow Sound, coiling rope, scraping paint
armed with my putty knife
and flare gun. I had my story
but forgot my tattoo. Kept the jacket on.
Stared, stared at the face in the bar. Oh, Chuck Luna,
you were back from the sea to order
a short one, thinner for the flu, discharged
for your mother, the only son in a family of sisters,
ready for a life of laying asphalt and good pay.

And though the ruddy-faced and aproned
barkeep knew, stubbed his smoke out,
and stared as I dribbled ten dollars in change all over his bar,
tilted my way past the pinballs, flush
with success, two cases of Oly
in my arms, and headed for the door leading back
to day after day, Chuck Luna,
I was still you.

SPLITTING WOOD

Who does he talk to
as he lifts the ax,
fists together,
and twists his shoulders
so gravity does the work,
so the blade cuts
sap-wet pine as neatly
as turning a page? Easy.
But his soaked hat
and jaw clenched the moment
wood falls back halved
into rain mean I cross-stack
split wood all day,
wondering as I have wondered
for years what he says
beneath his breath,
why his lips move as if
he reads by fingertip some badly
printed text. I have
never asked him
nor will I, groaning now
beneath my armful
of dead weight, my grip bad,
thinking if I'm to know
he'll tell me, the terms
certain, practiced, sharp enough
to lay open the heart
of those who strike him
worthy of love.

REUNION, CANNON BEACH

Tonight bats dive from blackness
through the streetlamp's bright skirt, plucking
moths from silver air before us,
my brother and me, who argue now whether
moths circle for warmth or light.
All the common ground we stood we
divided, our room staked off down the middle,
our yard a stage for scraps and too little
praise, each claiming the other
was favored, how the other started this all.
Tonight we drink to the ocean
close by and noisy, to the sand
between us brocaded with wild and fruitless
strawberries. We argue
over bats' catching in midair, over nothing,
sure of our differences, of the line
we draw down the middle of the room
our mother calls us into and we
separate as if such a move might leave us whole,
nestless, flown even from our father
who gave us different parts of his own name
or our mother who carries that picture
of one of us, out of focus, the face turned away,
whose rounded shoulders could
only be each of ours, though she still won't say
which of us it is.

A HAWK IN THE YARD

Pale, as tall as the thumb
at the length of my arm
before the tallest tree, a hawk
stalls, found out, skulking.
Now sparrows riot in the poplars,
now enterprise stops,
now the day brightens with fear
and noise, the wind having brought us
danger – there's a hawk in our yard,
preceded by his shadow
so we all knew of his coming,
so we all pay his tax of attention, eyes
forward, breath steady
in honor of what's in store someday
when we're not looking or fat
with supper or sick but not dead, just
our wakefulness gone, and
we find ourselves fleeing, winded
and slow, out into the open.
This is called revelation and giving
for which the hawk loves us all
one day and stoops, wings folded in adoration
of what he will enter talons first,
of what will sustain him.
But not today. Let him hop around
for locusts, dusty and awkward, found out
and a failure, wind-rumpled for
sitting so still above us, our fool
until he flies away.

NET

Stopped by the net tied
with twine up one side of your porch
over to and down the other,
an arch into which a summer's worth
of morning glories has drifted,
several bees and now me
caught a moment in this haul of blue petals,
this tangle of memory like a loose net
of blackberry canes. Once
full of impatience, I lay down
and saw far back the overlooked berries,
and for my reaching then, a swarm of bees, the sound
caught in my ears, and bees
everywhere for days in the least
wind or touch. Even now
the bumblebee that abandons one flower
for another frightens me
until it catches itself in a delicate blue seine.
I've learned to stand still.
On the other side laughter.
On this side entanglement, tendrils curling
around whatever they touch,
a daily cycle of blooming and twisting in currents
of air until the net lies green and heavy,
a full catch.

A STORY AFTER DINNER

Across the red and white tablecloth
a girl watches her grandfather drink another glass
of wine, the dinner over, crusts of bread
broken before her, the dishes stacked, talk scattered,
her mother within hearing – voices and water
running – and she gathers
empty glasses resplendent with cut leaves
and stems as fragile as new growth,
a few by her elbow, a copse to hide in, while
across a field her grandfather sits
back, suspenders loosened, watching through his glass
his granddaughter upside down above the white
table wine, waiting. A song? A story?
The long night of fires and lamps and memory,
names she has seen written, whose lives
she imagines given the date of birth
or death, a word or a rumor – all tied to her
across this field – wind caught in ash leaves speaking –
where her grandfather dips his fingers
into the last of the wine and circles the crystalline lip
until the glass hums, an announcement,
a single note released by his light touch and someone
still young enough to listen.

TWO MAGPIES

My father-in-law thought
one difference
between knowing and believing
was loving the quiet.
Another was two magpies
shot with his twelve-gauge resurrected
after sixty years of closets.
Who would believe the magpies
screeched only for him?
Full of lies we turned
our easy chairs to watch him
hit the first, stone-
dead, down in a litter of leaves,
then the second, startled,
clean on the fly. We turned back,
filled our glasses,
told ourselves there was hope
and it couldn't be.
He laid the shotgun down, broken
on the kitchen table.
No word, not a whisper,
he made for the bed
he would no longer rise from,
sure he'd taken the messengers with him,
sure he'd left us, the faithful
and nonbelieving,
a memory more troublesome
than a stone placed beneath our tongues
to make us listen.

JUST IN CASE

Is it the light
down the hall two hours
before morning or the mumbling
that wakes me?
You smoke in the kitchen, counters wiped,
the weights of the clock
drawn up to fall through
another day.

How you prepared all those summers
of pears and apples,
the washbaskets of cucumbers,
vigils beside the stove, a bandanna
tied around your head
as you waited for the holy ping
of pressure cooking.
I remember plenty, clothing
always clean just in case
and shoes that shamed me for growing.
It was no time to fiddle,
the ground turned over and mulched,
nickels in a jar.

You've done enough.
Home again, I saw Grandmother
in her bed, panting
beneath a cotton sheet too heavy
even to lift.
She could not hear.

And when the boy doctor
took you aside, I held her hand
and said nothing.
Pneumonia, he said. So easy it's kind.

Easy after years of water
boiled away, every burner on high,
your walls charred,
or the hip-breaking falls,
or letters to relatives,
detailing abuse. Take me away,
she wrote. There is no coffee here.

Mother, whatever you wished for
in the night-black window
has come true.
The kitchen is clean,
your silver put away.
I know you were given a hard choice
and took it,
unprepared as you were
to do nothing
when there's nothing left to do.

SNOW ANGEL

No, I'm saying the empty cicadas
I found one afternoon clinging to oak branches
were split down the back
as if the song I heard at night
was too shrill to be held any longer.

Sung to anger, I walked two flights down
late, and smoking, threw into the dark shoulder
of trees a stone that clattered
far away, a few cut leaves drifting to my feet
like wet indecipherable sheets of music.

Such urgency, this calling, like my mother's
when she sang out once, "Do you see?"
I have lied many times. Asleep or sad for myself,
the wipers methodical in the warm car
as my father drove, I said yes

and knew better, knew this day would be my history,
knew the hawk I hadn't seen was a word
I must fill with yellow eyes fixed on a boy
turning back into himself
behind his rain-blurred window. Give me clear sight

and I'll remember nothing.
Give me soot, the residue of bright burning,
and I'll trace the lost animals
of creation, articulate shadows, small emptinesses
driven into paper and lined with the color

that steals light. I'm saying
leaves fall and the smoke of their burning blossoms
in wind-sealed branches,
that my daughter has walked into the first snow
of winter and laid herself down to mimic

the shape of angels. How clumsy.
Such angels fall every day, the snow littered
with their absences. I'm saying
I found one day in drifts on a frozen pond
the intricate evidence of angels –

primary feathers packing shadows into snow,
the braking tail fanned out,
here the holy head, there the modest skirts pulled up
over a redeemed hare perhaps, an offering
to the heavenly trees. I would show my daughter the nothing left.

I would give her words to trace in snow,
a nothing wings might leave but she disagrees
already. Nonsense, she says, filling
the emptiness she rises up from with the sound
of her own name.

PART THREE

ORCHARD

The man who grew up there
every summer hung
a "peaches" sign two weeks early
and covered it with burlap so
each of us who drove
home after work might know
once again that peaches
were shortly in our future
and for the life of that season
we could stop and buy
a paper sack full. Maybe one-half
acre of trees – his father
had planted – the man weeded
and watered – twenty trees –
and pruned them and drove his tilt-
wheeled ancient John Deere
up and down the rows
twice to get the engine warm.
And the sound still
drifts and still it is the orange heart-
wood I remember one
spring when there was no sign
and he cut his trees down,
for they had lived past
blossoming, the man said,
and the stumps looked, if I squinted,
like fresh peaches cut
in half in summer dust and leaves.
Forty rings. For days

the burn piles filled the air
with smoke and when it lifted
the man had moved and I could see
where the trees had been
and where we had stopped
more clearly than before.

TREE OF HEAVEN

Not heaven enough.
Brittleness outside

creaks, a bough
splitting. We lie awake –

the moon flooding
our room – and wish

for summer, for leaves
lifting pale

undersides in so little breeze.
We were warned.

Soft wood litters
the yard. No eye bolts

and chain, no trimming
against the wind will do.

Soon starlings –
rain-slick, iridescent

in oiled feathers – will shake
the crooked branch

they leap from into flight.
One way or another

this tree must fall,
a name's failure,

a weed praised for its reaching,
its hallelujah of

new shoots
heaving the sidewalk up.

CONCERT

All winter sparrows
perch in hawthorns, not moving.
We walk by and stare
but do not reach out for the thorns,
for each other's hand.
Little by little exasperation
overtakes us – thought
and deed months apart.
Why do I think of refuge,
a child hiding beneath fir boughs,
wishing for rain?
We have come for music,
to sit closer than usual.
But first we walk to sharpen
the edge on our faces,
breath after breath a preoccupation,
temporary bloomings
on dark branches. Remember,
this has happened before –
our falling apart.
For days sparrows one
by one hide behind thorns.
It's the little I recall and why
we walk tonight,
the journey difficult
but clear and bright and cold.
We must return the way
we have come, past multitudes
of sparrows, their noisy hymn sung

for hunger and light.
Such chatter we walk through,
caught up for the moment
with ourselves.

PELICAN

How she sleeps. September's too hot &
storms fill the restaurants
with sand. From our balcony, *agua pura* &
limón on the short-legged tin table, my feet up,
I watch pelicans glide
thirty feet above the Bahía de Banderas, fishing,
storm or no storm. Would she laugh
if I say how I admire them,
if I describe a pelican
perched on my chair, its awkward lifting
into air, feet tucked up &
six-foot wings outstretched, gliding?
Would she love the turning
of a bald, featherless eye before
the pelican falls, wings folded, into the sea &
rises, a juggler of fish?
Or would she see that beak? That posture?
Some calligrapher's ampersand,
this bird that walks like a dead language?
Wake now. Let me try
to feather the edge of contradiction,
storm & calm, awkwardness if we wait,
unfolding into grace.

IN THE MIND'S EYE

There are blue and white shutters
nailed open and the glass
ground opaque by winter wind full
of sand. Before saw grass
and boardwalks, before the shingle,
before the sea rising into whitecaps, tell me,
are you there? I call and call.
Sometimes in late afternoon
on a bus maybe, clouds and blue sky wash up,
a sailboat heels over
out of reach, and I am awake in the blind morning,
the kettle whistling again
on the wood stove, the day warm already in summer, the island
waiting and the tide out
far enough to walk the beaches clear back
to where I started, a child rising
from breakfast and turning the brass knob
on the heavy door and stepping onto
the ever-growing shore. A passing
thought, all this? Where are you? Where
you took me rises like drift
on the tide and floats and resettles.
I see it now – wind, saw grass humming,
sand given to the air and air
washing my eyes.

FIRE LINE

In late August a tired man
rises culvert to road,
soot-masked, palms out to stop us,
to keep us from harm.
No harm. We watch wind
work fire through wheat stubble
and fences, posts
burnt off and falling back
into their wires.
We are driving home,
the road red beneath our fingers.
Wait. In the windshield
I see two faces stranded in a field on fire,
a crop duster's biplane,
full of retardant,
banking away from a hill, an eyebrow
wizened with flame.
I remember now
it's the dangerous flying
few speak of – not us
but the ancients who live here
with their red trucks
and contagious fire,
who pump the stream dry,
who let us run our course
with a wave of the hand
as if to say go, the road lies
burned clean both ways between shoulders
covered with ash.

SILVER THAW

After the sanctuary of night,
after the murder mystery read over and over
to find solace in every clue,
after the late-hour stumbling outside your door,
the broken glass, the moaning of the woman

who ignores you for her own pain,
so that you've known always what it is to be grown,
to live as mother to your own mother,
to love only the quiet of a night-blessed room
you would make, by choice, even smaller,

you rise this morning to find the windows frozen
as if breath you gave up last night
found shape and form, angular and perfect
like prehistoric ferns layered in stone.

And when you scrape them clean,
frost coating your fingers, the day enters
more brilliantly than you've ever remembered.
How much and how clearly you see,
each bud varnished with ice, the lawn shining
as if swollen with the making of light.

You think this is a day to begin,
that all you need is will, a passion for work,
a place found and named for everything
and everything in love with its name.
A day to end the life you've lived for others,

what you were frozen now in still air,
unshaken, unshakable by another's
silence or slur or inexplicable frown.
Today after dishes, after dusting,
after the bitter tea you wash your hands

and step outside into an indecision of weather,
night rain having fallen into frozen air,
a silver thaw where nothing moves or sings
and all things grieve under the weight
of their own shining.

DRIVING TO MULTNOMAH FALLS

In my lap lay
the blue river and when I looked up
from driving the water fell
so far away it seemed like feathers sewn
to a green housecoat
in morning light, a woman
leaning over children and the swell
of her breast beneath cotton – the sheer
embroidered cliff, part needle and pine stand
lay transformed. It doesn't help
to say the sun blinds.
In my mirrors geese flopped on a shoulder,
one waddling toward the river
as if nothing had happened. Smaller and smaller,
then nothing. I wish it were so.
What I bring with us aches.
We stopped to watch a silver train,
a flicker of windows and faces, and when
we stepped out to walk
a tunnel beneath the tracks, the earth moved
its quarter inch.
If I gave everything away –
myrtle wood, tumbled stones, pale
agates that comb particulars from the awful light –
would the boulders wear down
faster where we stand, our backs to shale, the cataract
before us? Light breaks up.
The water falls cold and pure enough
our hands go numb.
We tell each other we are grateful.

THE BLESSING OF HABIT

Tipped back, my hat
makes noise enough so they
unwrap their wings
too early in rafters. Yes,
it's their droppings
on the floor, dust-blown,
their shadows past our window
at dusk. At dawn. Found out,
I'm afraid. But outside
in light through the barn door,
through dust, in August,
I see that raspberries hang fat
on our side of the fence,
our tree sags with apples,
our house sits plumb
and nothing leaks.
Day after day we stand still
for each other, leaving
for work at morning,
then coming home, driven back to sit
beneath the box elder
that shades the barn, to drink
ice water at the edge
of evening. And because I wish
for long life and love virtue
and ask some nights,
curled against your familiar shape,
for a death as easy as leaves
dropping onto a roof,

into a yard to lie beneath snow,
I will burn no sulphur,
fix no barn window.
I will sweep the floor
and turn a blind eye in wonder
at what might prosper
in rafters in spring when the rains let up,
when we scrape and sand
and paint - in deference to bats –
the old barn red.

FIRST SNOW

At night I smell snow coming
and set out seed for birds,
wrap pipes, cut roses
back and bury them – all
the hard preparation
for air so cold the stars sit
as quiet as exhausted children.

The moon grows thin
on its diet of branches.

Then wood smoke
starts up morning, windows
iced over and wiped
back to their edges. Nothing out
but the yard so full
of light I squint, every shadow
taken. Once again
immaculate flakes drop
onto the steaming river,
onto my brow and tongue,
so the burden
of too many colors is lifted,
so I might lose
the poor horizon
and know the shape
of breath, the shiver
of understanding

that clean smell of snow
and green – for months ahead of me
only a memory.

QUARRY

No blasting now
but gentle work – the same thing
we fathers do for daughters. We bring them
one Saturday, warm for winter,
so they might get their fill of absence,
its clean lines and perfect faces.
And my first thought by the dangerous edge
is that we will leave them one day
an absence shaped like a father
or a single red leaf warmed by winter sun
and sinking through ice, the memory of itself
riding behind like a silhouette, a hand's weight
left on a shoulder, a kiss, a shadow
in the night-light, someone watching at the door.
Maybe. But explain this to daughters
who fill their hands with weeds and winter
flowers and square-stemmed mint and red hats
bobbing over fields below a house
empty and kneeling down beside this quarry
as if all played out. There's no one left
to count the crushed fingers.
The old bridge here has fallen, its limestone
abutments drifting, crossed now
only by sight. And I read later
the limestone blocks we sit our daughters on,
tons beneath flowers and faces,
were cut from good dimension stone, the parent ledge
they call it, and I know then our daughters
will leave us, their fathers, an absence, a word

to look back into like a quarry pond
warm all summer as we watch from the edge, waiting
for them to break the surface, breath
held, shaking their hair from those clean lines,
their perfect, unmarked faces.

DEAD RECKONING

The term disturbs me
as if to find the way back
is to reason with the dead.
I mean, it will save your life
even now as you walk
farther from me and stop
and turn, frightened a moment,
the land's lie strange,
the eucalyptus before you
disappearing into fog.

If you find me gone
or lost in thought, the long
tether of my eyes loosened,
I am years ago and two miles
at sea, my father steering
by compass through fog
opaque as newsprint. Listen.
Somewhere a horn groans in sleep
and I am terrified
by breakers that would drive us
onto black, barnacled stones.

I mean, he knew
how far and in which direction lay
the rickety dock, one road,
and the best cheapest restaurant
in Sekiu. I still hear
his blistered Evinrude missing,

the knock his razor made
against a bowl before the dawn's whistle
and our pushing off
into the calm, low-tide sea.

My daughter — born
into cold air and crying
before our voices called you
and you turned for home —
this is memory, a wind offshore
smelling of small towns
where fishermen walk the sea
out of their legs. Turn back now.

I will catch your eye and wave.
I mean, remember how far
and which way you have come.
I mean, go on where
I cannot follow.

RIDER

The horses have ruined the fields
this winter – too warm –
and over their fetlocks in mud,
steaming, they gather before the girl
who feeds them, for she is
of the fence and the green hay and of the sky-
blooming and if
they are far away she raps her tin bucket
and they run, for she
is of the grain and the wire brush and hoof pick.
Soon she will lead them
into the barn and pull their manes
and lay a knife along their backs to scrape
the winter coat away.
She has taught them to turn
at the window where the sparrows leap
with horse hair in their
beaks to rafters to nest and the dust
swirls. She has held
the horses' ears to stop them
and stung their flanks and barked
like the useless barn dog.
And when she fills their mouths and hooks
the keeper and straps and reaches
to lay on the blanket
and set the saddle behind their withers,
they stand still,
for she is of the tight bands
and the door rolled back.

She is part of the sky and part
of the dust and her hands clutch and she rises
and her legs spreading over back muscles
weigh no more than her word for canter or walk,
a cluck in the ear that means step
back into new grass
beneath the light that is she
each morning.

HOOKING YOURSELF

The moment you touch the shocked
rainbow beside the river you've fished
since dawn, your wife asleep in the car,
the hook flies loose . . .

Listen, there are ways to free yourself.
For skin toughened by misfortune,
elbows or the back of your hand,
use pliers on the hook's shank, grip hard,
and drive the barb back out where it came from.
For skin that tears like damp paper,
inside the wrist or along the throat, go on
with all you've started, cutting the eye clean
and pushing as if sewing one stitch,
point then barb before a thread of blood.
But if you've caught the lid of your eye
or any skin that loves what you hear or smell,

sit still, cut the line and think a moment
before you wake her. Sometimes there's no
saving yourself, such matters
right for the hands of your sleeping other.

THE IOWA POETRY PRIZE WINNERS

1987
Elton Glaser, *Tropical Depressions*
Michael Pettit, *Cardinal Points*

1988
Bill Knott, *Outremer*
Mary Ruefle, *The Adamant*

1989
Conrad Hilberry, *Sorting the Smoke*
Terese Svoboda, *Laughing Africa*

1993
Tom Andrews, *The Hemophiliac's Motorcycle*
Michael Heffernan, *Love's Answer*
John Wood, *In Primary Light*

1994
James McKean, *Tree of Heaven*
Bin Ramke, *Massacre of the Innocents*
Ed Roberson, *Voices Cast Out to Talk Us In*

THE EDWIN FORD PIPER POETRY AWARD WINNERS

1990
Philip Dacey, *Night Shift at the Crucifix Factory*
Lynda Hull, *Star Ledger*

1991
Greg Pape, *Sunflower Facing the Sun*
Walter Pavlich, *Running near the End of the World*

1992
Lola Haskins, *Hunger*
Katherine Soniat, *A Shared Life*